D1510678

Machines at Work

Cranes

by Wendy Strobel Dieker

Bullfrog
Books

Ideas for Parents and Teachers

Bullfrog Books let children practice reading informational text at the earliest reading levels. Repetition, familiar words, and photo labels support early readers.

Before Reading:
- Discuss the cover photo. What does it tell them?

- Look at the picture glossary together. Read and discuss the words.

Read the Book
- "Walk" through the book and look at the photos. Let the child ask questions. Point out the photo labels.

- Read the book to the child, or have him or her read independently.

After Reading
- Prompt the child to think more. What kinds of cranes have you seen? What were they helping to build?

Bullfrog Books are published by Jump!
5357 Penn Avenue South
Minneapolis, MN 55419
www.jumplibrary.com

Library of Congress Cataloging-in-Publication Data
Dieker, Wendy Strobel.
 Cranes / by Wendy Strobel Dieker.
   p. cm. — (Bullfrog books. Machines at work)
 Audience: K to grade 3
 Summary: "This photo-illustrated book for early readers describes the parts of a crane, different types of cranes, and the jobs they do. Includes picture glossary"—Provided by publisher.
 Includes bibliographical references and index.
 ISBN 978-1-62031-018-2 (hardcover : alk. paper)
 1. Cranes, derricks, etc.--Juvenile literature. I. Title.
 TJ1363.D526 2013
 621.8'73—dc23   2012008572

Series Editor: Rebecca Glaser
Series Designer: Ellen Huber
Photo Researcher: Heather Dreisbach

Photo Credits: 123rf, 20; Alamy, 21; Dreamstime.com, 9; Getty Images, 12–13; iStockphoto, cover, 10–11, 12; Shutterstock, 1, 3, 4, 5, 8, 14–15, 15, 22, 23tl, 23br; SuperStock, 18–19, 23bl; Veer, 6–7, 16–17, 23tr, 24

Printed in the United States of America at Corporate Graphics, North Mankato, Minnesota.
7-2012 / PO 1122
10 9 8 7 6 5 4 3 2 1

Table of Contents

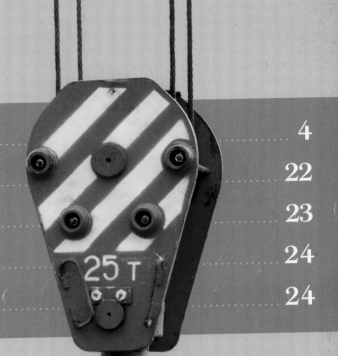

Cranes at Work

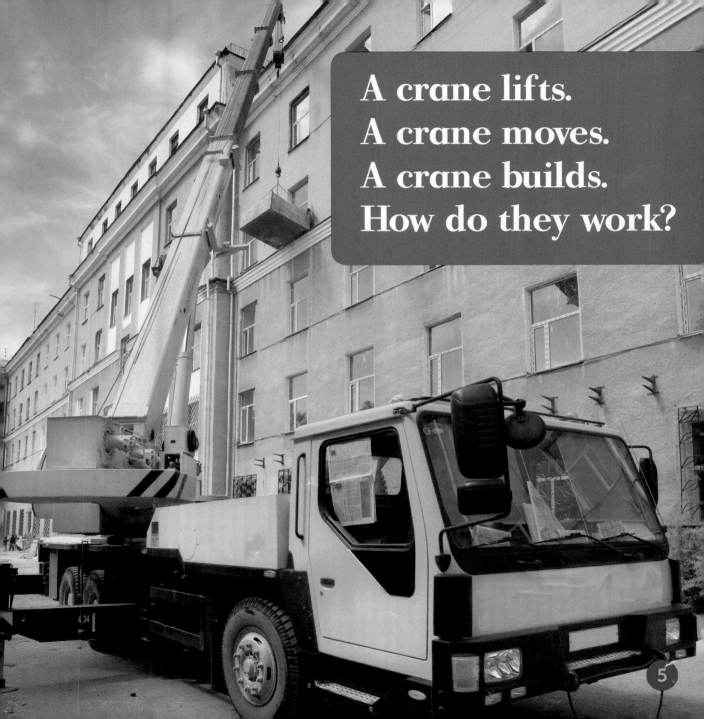

A crane lifts.
A crane moves.
A crane builds.
How do they work?

5

Look up!
A crane has a boom.
It is like an arm.
It goes side to side.

boom

A crane has a cable.
It goes up and down.
It is strong!

cable

A crane has a pulley.
The cable goes around it.
A pulley makes it easy to lift.

pulley

hook

Look!
A crane has a hook.
It picks up things.

A crawler crane
has tracks.

It moves slowly.

It helps build a road.

tracks

15

A tower crane is tall.
It helps build a hotel.
It reaches up 25 floors.

16

Do you hear that?

It is a sky crane.
It helps build a tower.

A crane is good at lifting!

Parts of a Crane

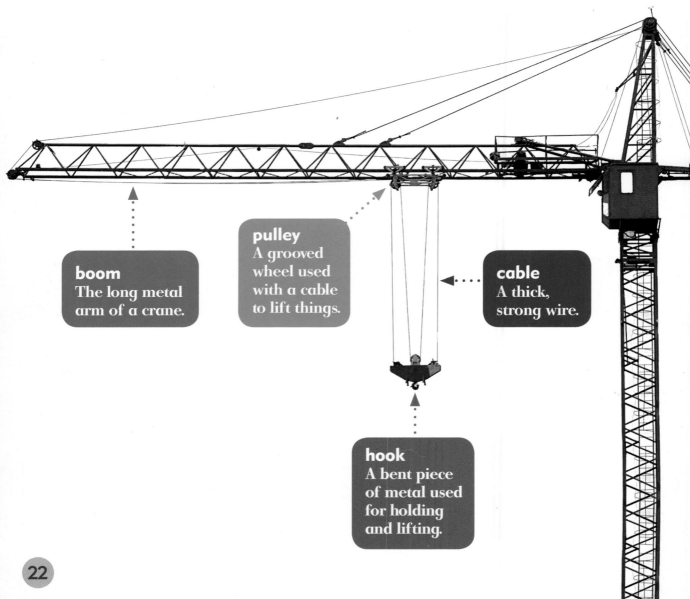

boom
The long metal arm of a crane.

pulley
A grooved wheel used with a cable to lift things.

cable
A thick, strong wire.

hook
A bent piece of metal used for holding and lifting.

Picture Glossary

crawler crane
A crane with large tracks that moves on the ground.

tower crane
A crane built next to a building; it does not drive around; some are built on top of tall buildings.

sky crane
A helicopter used for heavy lifting.

tracks
Rubber with ridges that goes around wheels so they don't sink into mud.

Index

To Learn More

Learning more is as easy as 1, 2, 3.

1) Go to www.factsurfer.com

2) Enter "crane" into the search box.

3) Click the "Surf" button to see a list of websites.

With factsurfer.com, finding more information is just a click away.